I'm finally up to double digits in the volumes. Thank you to all the readers who have stuck with me since the beginning. To all the readers who just recently started, welcome. This is ***World Trigger*** volume 10.

—**Daisuke Ashihara, 2015**

Daisuke Ashihara began his manga career at the age of
en his manga ***Room 303*** won second place in the
ezuka Awards. His first series, ***Super Dog Rilienthal***,
serialization in ***Weekly Shonen Jump*** in 2009.
Trigger is his second serialized work in ***Weekly***
en Jump. He is also the author of several shorter
including the one-shots ***Super Dog Rilienthal***,
r Keeper and ***Elite Agent Jin***.

WORLD TRIGGER VOL. 10
SHONEN JUMP Manga Edition

STORY AND ART BY DAISUKE ASHIHARA

Translation/Lillian Olsen
Touch-Up Art & Lettering/Annaliese Christman
Design/Sam Elzway
Weekly Shonen Jump Editor/Hope Donovan
Graphic Novel Editor/Marlene First

Printed in the U.S.A.

Published by VIZ Media, LLC
P.O. Box 77010
San Francisco, CA 94107

10 9 8 7 6 5 4 3 2 1
First printing, May 2016

www.viz.com

PARENTAL ADVISORY
WORLD TRIGGER is rated T for Teen and is recommended for ages 13 and up. This volume contains fantasy violence.
ratings.viz.com

www.shonenjump.com

SHONEN JUMP MANGA EDITION

10

WORLD TRIGGER

DAISUKE ASHIHARA

WORLD TRIGGER DATA BASE

Invasion NEIGHBOR

Invaders from another dimension that enter Mikado City through Gates. Most "Neighbors" here are Trion soldiers built for war. The Neighbors who actually live on the other side of the Gates are human, like Yuma.

Trion soldier built for war. ▶

AFTOKRATOR

The largest military nation in the Neighbor world, reported to have seven Black Triggers 13 years ago. They are invading Earth to kidnap people with Trion abilities.

HYREIN

Captain. Uses the Black Trigger Alektor that turns people into cubes.

MIRA

Uses a Black Trigger that makes wormholes. Mercilessly kills allies when ordered to.

VIZA

Uses Aftokrator's national treasure, Organon. Lost to Yuma and Replica.

HYUSE

Uses magnetized shards called Lambiris. Fighting Jin.

ENEDORA

Uses the Black Trigger Borboros, which liquefies his body. Attacked Border HQ and lost.

RANBANEIN

Uses the shooting Trigger Keridon. Lost to Izumi, Yoneya and Midorikawa.

Horns

Aftokrator produces humans with exceptional Trion abilities by implanting Trigger-equipped Trion receptors into their heads. A horned person's fighting abilities far exceed that of a normal Trigger user's. Some horns are compatible with Black Triggers, which turn the horns black.

BORDER

An agency founded to protect the city's peace from Neighbors. Agents are classified as follows: C-Rank for trainees, B-Rank for main forces, A-Rank for elites and S-Rank for those with Black Triggers. A-Rank squads get to go on away missions to Neighbor worlds.

Resistance

C-Rank: Chika

B-Rank: Osamu

A-Rank: Arashiyama Squad, Miwa Squad

Trigger

A technology created by Neighbors to manipulate Trion. Used mainly as weapons, Triggers come in various types. Border classifies them into three groups: Attacker, Gunner, and Sniper.

▲Attacker Trigger

▲Gunner Trigger

◀Sniper Trigger

Black Trigger

A special Trigger created when a skilled user pours their entire life force and Trion into a Trigger. Outperforms regular Triggers, but the user must be compatible with the personality of the creator, meaning only a few people can use any given Black Trigger.

▲Yuma's father Yugo sacrificed his life to create a Black Trigger and save Yuma.

STORY

About four years ago, a Gate connecting to another dimension opened in Mikado City, leading to the appearance of invaders called Neighbors. After the establishment of the Border Defense Agency, people were able to return to their normal lives.

Osamu Mikumo is a junior high student who meets Yuma Kuga, a Neighbor. Yuma is targeted for capture by Border, but Tamakoma branch agent Yuichi Jin steps in to help. He convinces Yuma to join Border instead, then gives his Black Trigger to HQ in exchange for Yuma's enlistment. Now Osamu, Yuma and Osamu's friend Chika work toward making A-Rank together.

Another large-scale Neighbor attack on Mikado City begins. Their horned appearance reveals that they are from Aftokrator, the largest military nation in the Neighborhood. Border defeats Enedora and his Black Trigger after he invades HQ. Viza loses to Yuma and Replica. The future is looking much better for Border and Mikado City. Meanwhile, Hyrein continues to pursue the cubified Chika and destroys Replica! Miwa comes to the rescue but is immediately transported far away. What will Osamu do?!

WORLD TRIGGER CHARACTERS

TAMAKOMA BRANCH

Understanding toward Neighbors. Considered divergent from Border's main philosophy.

TAKUMI RINDO

Tamakoma Branch Director

CHIKA AMATORI

Osamu's childhood friend. She has high Trion levels.

YUMA KUGA

A Neighbor who carries a Black Trigger.

OSAMU MIKUMO

Ninth-grader who's compelled to help those in trouble. B-Rank Border agent.

TAMAKOMA-1

Tamakoma's A-Rank squad.

REIJI KIZAKI

KYOSUKE KARASUMA

KIRIE KONAMI

SHIORI USAMI

REPLICA

Yuma's chaperone.

YUICHI JIN

Former S-Rank Black Trigger user. His Side Effect lets him see the future.

SUWA SQUAD HQ B-Rank No. 8 squad.

KOTARO SUWA

DAICHI TSUTSUMI

HISATO SASAMORI

IZUHO NATSUME

C-Rank trainee hoping to become a sniper. Chika's friend.

ARAFUNE SQUAD HQ B-Rank No. 10 all-Sniper squad.

TETSUJI ARAFUNE

ATSUSHI HOKARI

YOSHITO HANZAKI

BORDER HQ

MASAMUNE KIDO

HQ Commander

MASAFUMI SHINODA

HQ Director, Defense Force Commander

EIZO NETSUKI

PR Director

KATSUMI KARASAWA

Business Director

MOTOKICHI KINUTA

R&D Director

WORLD TRIGGER

CONTENTS

Chapter 80 Replica: Part 3

THE HUMANOID NEIGHBOR!
WHAT HAPPENED TO MIWA?!

BUT... I CAN DO THIS!

IT'S CLOSE ENOUGH...
...THAT I CAN JUST BARELY MAKE IT.

ZAP

I'LL GATHER MY REMAINING ATTACK TRION.
VWEEEM

IT'S MY DUTY...
...TO STOP THE CARRIER!!

SHK
SHK
SHK

ZHUNK
...!!
GAH ...!!
I CAUGHT UP.
WELL DONE, MIRA.
I'M SO CLOSE...!!

OSAMU.
THROW ME!
...!

HOWEVER, IF IT'S A NEIGHBOR SYSTEM...
...I CAN ANALYZE AND OVERRIDE IT INSTANTLY.
...!
YOU MEAN YOU WANT TO ATTACK THE NEIGHBOR SHIP!
I CANNOT GUARANTEE YOUR SURVIVAL, SINCE THIS WOULD BE BEYOND JIN'S FORESIGHT.
BUT ALONG-SIDE YOUR PLAN...
...IT IS HIGHLY PROBABLE WE CAN PROTECT CHIKA.
HIS AIM...
...IS OUR SHIP!

BLAM BLAM

BLAM

...IS THE ONE WHO DEFEATED VIZA.

*Seals: Strength, Shoot (x2)

...I WON'T HAVE ANY TROUBLE KILLING THE CARRIER!

SLA
SH
OOO
A DIRECT HIT.
SHF

SLASH
?!
A SLASH ATTACK!
WHERE DID THAT—

...
NGH!
RAAAAAH!

FL ING
BEEP
INFILTRATION-
COMPLETE.

RRRRMMMM

!!

COM-MANDER!

CHECK THE SHIP!

A RETURN HOME COMMAND HAS BEEN ISSUED!

ONLY SIXTY SECONDS UNTIL EMER-GENCY LAUNCH!

AND THEY TARGETED THE SHIP...

...SO WE WOULDN'T HAVE TIME TO SEARCH FOR THE **REAL** ONE!

...

WE HAVE NO CHOICE.

WE WILL GIVE UP ON THE GOLDEN GOOSE.

CAN YOU MOVE THE SHIP'S GATE BEFORE LAUNCH?

YES!

I WILL RECOVER MR. VIZA!

AND HYUSE...

WHAT SHOULD I DO ABOUT HIM?

AH, YES...

SINCE THE GOLDEN GOOSE GOT AWAY...

...WE WILL LEAVE HYUSE HERE...

...AS PLANNED.

...

OSAMU.

RRRMMMM
THIS IS GOODBYE.
TAKE CARE OF YUMA.
MM

...?!
REPLICA ?!
PLOP
?!
PLOP
VWEEEEE
ZZK

HUH?
THE SKY'S CLEARED ?!

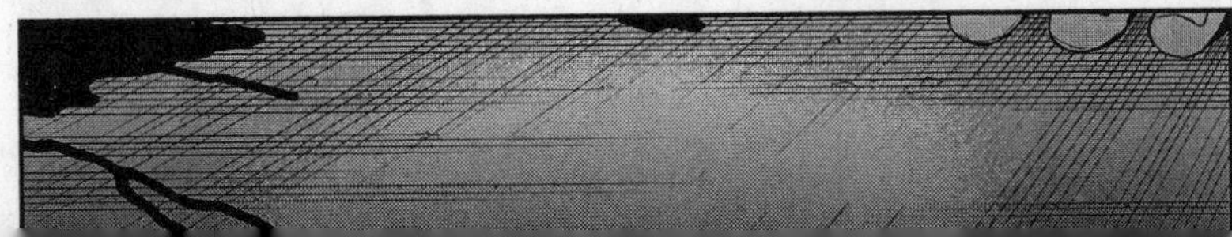

W RLD
TRIGGER

Chapter 81 Invasion: Part 24

WOOOO

BOOM
SKK
WAAH
!!
NEIGHBORS ARE COMING!
WAAAH
EEEK !!
SHH

...!
THEY'RE TOO SPREAD OUT.
I CAN'T COVER THEM ALL BY MYSELF.
KSH
KSH
KSH
BLAM BLAM
?!

SORRY FOR THE LONG WAIT, PEOPLE OF MIKADO!
NOW THAT KEN SATORI, THE PEERLESS DOUBLE-SHOT SNIPER, IS ON THE SCENE...
KWEEM
HM...?
BOOM
WAH!!
YOU JERK!

BLAM
ZING
KRAK
SLASH
LOOK!
IT'S ARASHI-YAMA SQUAD!!
ARASHI-YAMA SQUAD IS HERE!

JUN!
JIN TOLD US TO COME LEND A HAND!
WELL DONE HOLDING THEM OFF BY YOURSELF, KIRIE!
TA-DA
KONAMI!
DIDJA SEE MY ACROBATIC DOUBLE SNIPE?
YES, I SAW.
KONAMI.
I HEAR YOU SAVED KITORA. THANK YOU.
SHE'S STILL A CUBE, BUT SHE'S RIGHT HERE.
ALONG WITH THE TRAINEES.
LET'S WIPE THE REST OF THEM OUT QUICKLY!
THAT WAY THE DAMAGE TO THE CITY WILL BE MINIMIZED!

KDSH
!
TOO BAD...
LOOKS LIKE THE PARTY'S OVER.
WE'RE TOO LATE.
THOOM
A 06
K
KAKO SQUAD
A-RANK #6
(ALL-GIRLS SQUAD)

A 06
K
NOZOMI KAKO (20)
CAPTAIN, SHOOTER
A 06
K
FUTABA KUROE (13)
ATTACKER
KAKO!
KIRIE, ARASHI-YAMA.
LEAVE THIS TO US.
WE'LL MAKE UP FOR LOST TIME.
LET'S DO THIS.
FUTABA.
OKAY!

WOOOOO

THE HUMANOID NEIGHBORS HAVE WITHDRAWN!
OSAMU IS UNCONSCIOUS AND IN SERIOUS CONDITION!
CHIKA MADE IT INSIDE THE BASE!

PHEEEW!

FWUMP
?!

IT'S ALL RIGHT NOW.
SIGH
THEY'RE BOTH SAFE.

FOUR-EYES WILL LIVE.
REALLY ?!
OH, THANK GOOD-NESS!

IT'S ALL THANKS TO PROFESSOR REPLICA...

...
WHY, YOU...!!

SORRY I HAD TO STALL YOU.
OUR YOUNGER MEMBERS WERE GOING TO BE IN DANGER IF I LET YOU WANDER.

BUT I THINK...
...IT'S A GOOD THING YOU STAYED ON THIS SIDE.

THERE'S SOMETHING GOING ON, RIGHT?
THAT'S WHAT MY SIDE EFFECT TELLS ME.

...!
THIS MAN...

VRRM

THERE'S NO REASON FOR US TO FIGHT ANYMORE.
I SUGGEST YOU SUR-RENDER.
YOU WON'T BE TREATED BADLY.

HMM?
WHERE IS HYUSE?

WE FAILED TO CAPTURE THE GOLDEN GOOSE.
WE CAN'T TAKE HYUSE BACK WITH US.

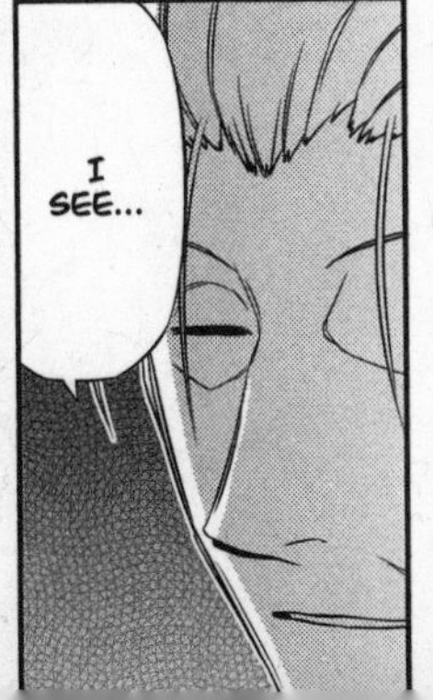
I SEE...

IT'S A PITY.
HE WAS SO TALENTED...
THIS WAS ALWAYS THE PLAN.
IF WE TOOK HIM BACK, HE WOULD BECOME OUR ENEMY.

MAN, WHAT A WASTE.
IF ONLY WE'D GOTTEN THE GOLDEN GOOSE.

GLARE
OOPS...

PERHAPS I WAS IMPATIENT.
NO...
THOSE CONDITIONS ...
...AND THE ENEMY POSITIONS...

AN UNANTICI-PATED ENEMY...
THE DELAY BEFORE ENEMY REINFORCE-MENTS ARRIVED...

VIZA'S UNEXPECTED DEFEAT...
THE CARRIER'S TRIGGER DEACTI-VATION ...

IT FEELS MORE LIKE...
...SOMEONE SET THE CARDS TO FALL LIKE THAT.

THE MISSION IS OVER.
REST UNTIL WE GET BACK TO OUR HOME COUNTRY.
IT'S TOO BAD THE GOLDEN GOOSE GOT AWAY, BUT...

REGARDING ENEDORA AND HYUSE...
...OUR ORIGINAL OBJECTIVES HAVE BEEN MET.

EAST OF HQ
TACHIKAWA HERE.
I'VE DISPOSED OF ALL THE NEIGHBORS.
BUT SOME TRAINEES ARE STILL MISSING.
A BUNCH OF THEM MUST'VE GOTTEN KIDNAPPED BEFORE I GOT HERE.
SOUTH OF HQ
HQ.
WE'RE ALSO MISSING IS TRAINEES.
THEY WERE TAKEN WHILE WE WERE DEALING WITH THE HUMANOIDS.
WE'VE HUNTED DOWN THE REMAINING ENEMIES.
B-RANK SQUADS WILL NOW ASSIST THE CIVILIANS.

...!
URGH...!

THERE'S A LOT OF DAMAGE.
THE HUMANOIDS MESSED EVERY-THING UP!

SINCE AGENTS WERE KIDNAPPED...
...IT'S INEVITABLE THAT THE CITIZENS WILL HOUND US...

...

MR. KIDO.

THERE WON'T BE ANY MORE ENEMY ATTACKS.
IT'S SAFE TO SEND MEDICAL TEAMS TO THE EAST AND THE SOUTH.

Border Losses

Deaths: 6 (all Operators in the Communications Center)
Serious injuries: 4
Missing: 32 (all C-Rank trainees)

Civilian Losses

Deaths: 0
Serious injuries: 22
Minor injuries: 68

EVERYONE DID VERY WELL.

I SEE...
ALL RIGHT...
WELL DONE.

Neighbor Losses
Deaths: 1 (by a fellow Neighbor)
Captured: 1
The battle to defend Mikado City from the Neighbor invasion...
...is over.

Kako Squad

Border HQ A-Rank #6

Nozomi Kako
Captain, Shooter

■20 years old (College student)
■Born Dec. 25

■Clavis, Blood type B
■Height: 5′8″
■Likes: Driving, apples, cooking fried rice, talented people

Futaba Kuroe
Attacker

■13 years old (Middle school student)
■Born Nov. 30

■Cetacea, Blood type B
■Height: 4′8″
■Likes: Rice dumplings with sweet red bean paste, tangerines, winning Rank Wars

Mai Kitagawa
Trapper

■16 years old (High school student)
■Born Feb. 28

■Apis, Blood type B
■Height: 5′1″
■Likes: Boiled tofu, kotatsu, drawing

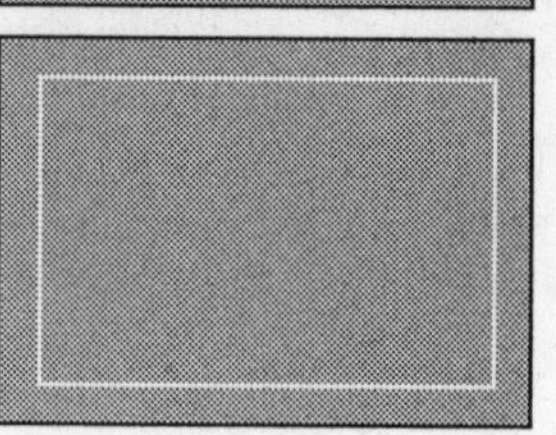

An Kobayakawa
Operator

■16 years old (High school student)
■Born Jan. 10

■Clavis, Blood type AB
■Height: 5′2″
■Likes: Black globe grapes, food fried with seaweed, reading, dogs

Chapter 82 Osamu Mikumo: Part 9

CRMBL
CRMBL
THERE YOU GO! COME ON OUT!

WE DID IT!
WAAAAH
EVERYONE'S FINALLY BEEN RESCUED!

GOOD JOB HANGING IN THERE.

THANK YOU!
THAT WAS AMAZING!
NAH.

I'M PRETTY COMFORTABLE WITH PHYSICAL STUFF.
I USED TO PLAY RUGBY IN SCHOOL.
KATSUMI KARASAWA (33)
BORDER
BUSINESS DIRECTOR

MIKADO CITY GENERAL HOSPITAL
Chapter 82 Osamu Mikumo: Part 9

BIP
BIP
BIP

BIP

OSAMU ...!
DON'T DIE, OSAMU!
WAAAH...

HE'LL BE FINE.
JIN SAYS HE WON'T DIE.

SO...
WHERE'S YUMA?

HE WAS HERE...
...BUT HE JUST WENT OUTSIDE.

HE SAID HE WAS GOING TO LOOK FOR REPLICA.
I SEE.

WE STILL HAVE A FEW MORE DAYS BEFORE THE ENEMY PLANET DRIFTS AWAY.
EVEN THOUGH THE OFF-DUTY AGENTS ARE MOSTLY BACK NOW...
...WE'RE NOT OUT OF THE WOODS YET.

OKAY!
ROGER.

THIS IS GOODBYE.
WHERE'S YUMA?
OSAMU.
SHOW ME HOW YOU'VE IMPROVED SINCE THE LAST TIME.
I TRUST YOU'LL TAKE CARE OF THE MARMOD.
DON'T DEPEND ON OTHERS.
RUN, OSAMU!
IN...
YOU PROTEC
WITH OUR LIFE.
IF THERE'S EVEN A SMALL POSSIBILITY, I...
DO WE HAVE ACTUAL VISITORS?
FIGHTING WITH WISDOM AND CREATIVITY.
CAN YOU KEEP GOING?
CONGRATS ON YOUR PROMOTION TO B-RANK!
YOU CAN LEAVE NOW.
BECAUSE
...THAT'S THE WAY I THINK IT SHOULD BE.
WELL DONE!!
IS THAT SO?!
WELL
I'M ASKING HIM TO JOIN OUR BRANCH.
I'M NOT TAKING HIM TO HQ.

RINJI... WHAT'S THIS?
A TRIGGER.
IT'S A BORDER WEAPON.
I MADE A DEAL TO GET IT.
A DEAL... WITH WHOM?
SOMEONE AT BORDER?
I HAVE TO KEEP MY COLLABORATORS' IDENTITIES A SECRET.
THOSE COLLABORATORS AND I...
...ARE GOING TO SEE WHAT'S BEYOND A NEIGHBOR GATE.
BEYOND A GATE?
NEIGHBORS COME TO THIS SIDE THROUGH DIMENSIONAL GATES.
SO HOW DO THEY GET BACK?
FWAP
THERE MUST BE A **RETURN GATE** TO BRING KIDNAPPED PEOPLE THROUGH...
...OR SOMETHING LIKE AN ENTRANCE TO A NEIGHBOR SPACESHIP.

WE HAVE AN IDEA...

...WHERE ONE MIGHT BE.

IF YOU DESTROY IT...

...WILL THE NEIGHBORS STOP COMING?

THEN CHIKA COULD STOP...

...RUNNING AWAY AND HIDING ON HER OWN!

DON'T BE CRAZY.
WE MIGHT DIE OR GET CAPTURED.
YOUR PARENTS WOULD NEVER FORGIVE ME IF THAT WERE TO HAPPEN TO YOU.
BUT THAT GOES FOR YOU TOO...
IT'S NOT THE SAME.
I'LL BE HONEST.
YOU'RE NOT CUT OUT FOR THIS STUFF.
YOU'LL GET YOURSELF KILLED.
...!!
...
...
SIGH
...
THINK ABOUT IT CAREFULLY.
WE'LL BE GOING NEXT SATURDAY.
APRIL 28 (SUN)
CALL ME IF YOU THINK YOU'RE UP FOR IT.
OKAY...

MAY 2 (THURS)
FSSH
...EVIDENCE THAT THEY USED A TRIGGER...
...REMAINS HAVEN'T BEEN FOUND...
FSSHH

MAY
OSAMU!
CHIKA!
MY BROTHER ...
HE'S GONE!
IT'S MY FAULT!
WAAAAH!!
...SO THEY WERE PROBABLY CAPTURED...
OSAMU.
I SET THIS EMAIL TO REACH YOU TOMORROW.
IF YOU'RE READING THIS MESSAGE ...
...IT MEANS I DIDN'T COME BACK.
Osamu.
I set this email
to reach you
tomorrow.

I'M SORRY I TRICKED YOU.
BUT I COULDN'T TAKE YOU WITH US.
YOU'RE TOO EARNEST AND HONORABLE.

DON'T PUSH YOURSELF.
STAY BY CHIKA'S SIDE.

THAT WAS THE FIRST TIME...

...I EVER SAW CHIKA CRY.

BORDER ENLISTMENT EXAM HALL
10AM Basic Scholastic Aptitude Test
1PM Physical Fitness Test
3PM Interviews
THE APTITUDE TEST WILL BEGIN IN FIVE MINUTES.
PLEASE TAKE YOUR ASSIGNED SEATS.
RESULTS WILL BE POSTED ON THE FIRST FLOOR BULLETIN BOARD.
ACCEPTANCE LIST
0001 0018
0002 0021
0004 0022
0005 0027
0009 0028
IF YOU SEE YOUR NUMBER, PLEASE GET YOUR PAPERS FROM THE STAFF.
OSAMU MIKUMO
UMBER 0019

SO... MIKUMO, WAS IT? I TAKE IT...
...YOU'RE NOT SATISFIED WITH THE RESULTS?
WELL... IT'S NOT THAT...
I DON'T THINK MY EXAM RESULTS COULD'VE BEEN THAT BAD...
HM... YOU HAVE A PROBLEM WITH THE ACCEPTANCE CRITERIA.
IT'S NOT JUST ABOUT THE THINGS THAT ARE OBVIOUS.
THE BIGGEST CRITERION, IN SHORT...
...IS THE APTITUDE TO USE A TRIGGER.
APTITUDE ...
WELL, YOU MIGHT NOT BE ABLE TO UNDERSTAND WHAT IT IS.
BUT DISTINCT DIFFERENCES IN ABILITY DO EXIST.
EVEN NOW, THIS ROOM IS MEASURING YOUR APTITUDE.
I'M AFRAID...
...IT'LL BE DIFFICULT FOR YOU TO BE AN AGENT.
WHAT ABOUT BEING AN ENGINEER OR AN OPERATOR?
BORDER IS KEPT AFLOAT BY MANY IMPORTANT SUPPORT STAFF.
...

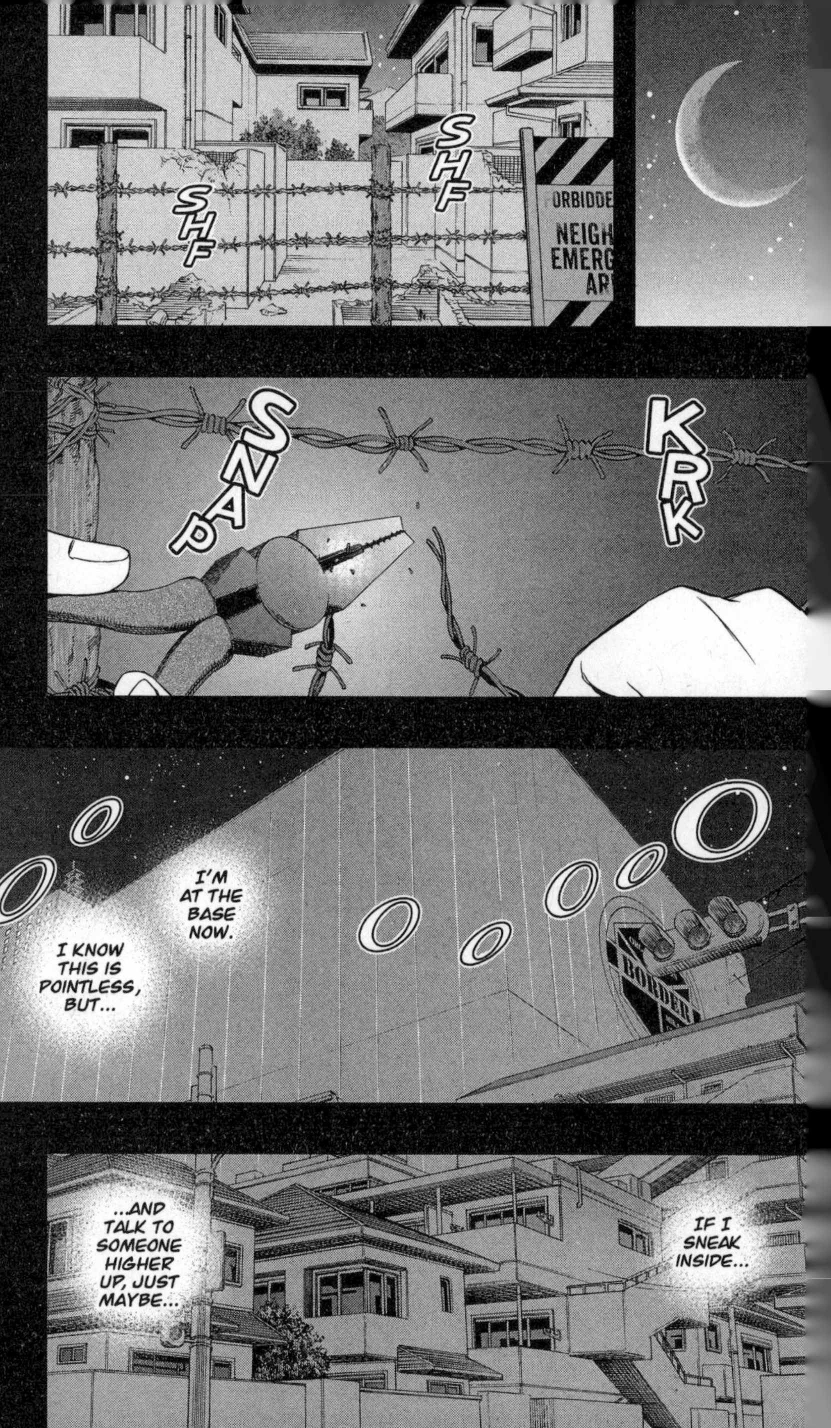
SHF
SHF
KRK
SNAP
I'M AT THE BASE NOW.
I KNOW THIS IS POINTLESS, BUT...
BORDER
IF I SNEAK INSIDE...
...AND TALK TO SOMEONE HIGHER UP, JUST MAYBE...

GATE DETECTED.
ZAP
...?!
WEEEEOOOOOM
COORDINATES MARGIN OF ERROR: 0.11.
RR DR
M M M
?!
IT'S HUGE...
A NEIGH-BOR?!
T
OH NO.
IT'S GOING TO EAT
US

HEY.
YOU ALL RIGHT, FOUR-EYES?

A DREAM...

MIKADO CITY GENERAL HOSPITAL
EMERGENCY ROOM
MOM...

Q&A: Part 9

I've been too busy for this for a while.

■Does anyone live at the Tamakoma branch?

Director Rindo, Yotaro, Jin and Reiji do. Everyone has their own private rooms though, and Konami and Usami routinely spend the night there. Osamu, Yuma and Chika's rooms will be ready soon.

■Okudera used a Full-Guard in the battle against Ranbanein, but can you use other Triggers if the Kogetsu is still out but in its scabbard?

You can turn off the Kogetsu even without putting it in its scabbard, but it won't be able to cut anything. When you use it, you can't put it away, so it's really annoying. You can abandon it and rebuild it and use it again, but you'll just consume Trion like with the gun Triggers.

■Does the Trion organ decrease with age?

If you don't use it, it will gradually wear out. It can be maintained if you keep using it.

■What's Osamu's favorite recipe his mother makes?

Cream croquettes. She makes them from scratch, including the béchamel sauce.

■Are all agents from Mikado?

Basically, but they do recruit from other prefectures. There are a few nonlocals.

■What do you call the Trion cubes that Shooters use?

Trion cubes, nata de coco, sugar cubes, Suwa, tofu, etc. Whatever you want really.

■Can a Hound follow someone who is using a Chameleon? Does it show up on radar?

A guided Hound can follow, but they usually get blocked by walls. They show up on radar in spy mode, so you can bomb the general area.

■Yuma's C-Rank uniform was black...did Jin arrange that?

It's the design established by Yugo, Yuma's father, long ago. It's a relic from the old Border days.

■Why was Suwa smoking a cigarette as a Trion body?

To look cool. There weren't any ashtrays, so they might not have been real cigarettes.

I sometimes answer questions I get in my fan mail on my official Twitter feed. When I get more followers, nobody can stop my editor. **World Trigger Official Twitter Account: @W_Trigger_off**

Chapter 83
Yuma Kuga: Part 10

YOU WERE BADLY HURT...
...BUT CHIKA DIDN'T CRY FOR YOU.
THE TWO OF YOU AREN'T INTIMATE ENOUGH.
YOU NEED TO GET CLOSER.
...

JAN 27 MON
PM 10 57
THE 27TH...
I WAS OUT FOR MORE THAN A WEEK...

ANYBODY ELSE?

YOU WERE ALSO VISITED BY THE BORDER HQ DIRECTOR...
AND PEOPLE I DON'T KNOW, BUT HAVE SEEN ON TV.

ALSO AN EARNEST YOUNG MAN...
BLIP
AND A VERY POLITE YOUNG LADY.
BLIP

AND...A YOUNGER GIRL?
BLIP
AND A YOUNGER BOY...
BLIP

...WITH BLACK HAIR AND SHARP EYES.
BLIP
...

A LIVELY TRIO OF BOYS ALSO CAME.
That's his mom?!
Not his sister?!
So young!!

ON THE OTHER HAND...
A BOY NAMED JIN FROM TAMAKOMA CAME HERE IN LOW SPIRITS.
HE KEPT APOLOGIZING TO ME AND CHIKA.
JIN?

... MM ...
HM?

OH... OSAMU!
YOU'RE AWAKE.
I'M SO GLAD!
CHIKA.

ARE YOU OKAY?
IT STILL HURTS, BUT...
HEY, CHIKA...

WHERE'S KUGA?

...!
KUGA?
I HAVEN'T MET HIM.
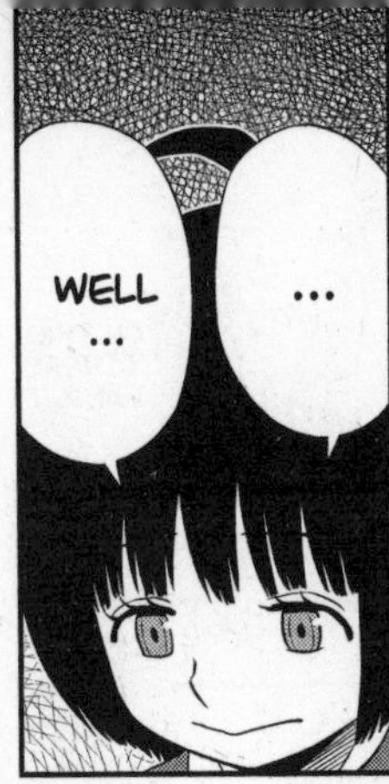
...
WELL ...

HE HASN'T VISITED FOR A WHILE...
...!

BUT...
ONCE HE HEARS THAT YOU'RE AWAKE...
...I'M SURE HE'LL COME TOMORROW!

...
I SEE...
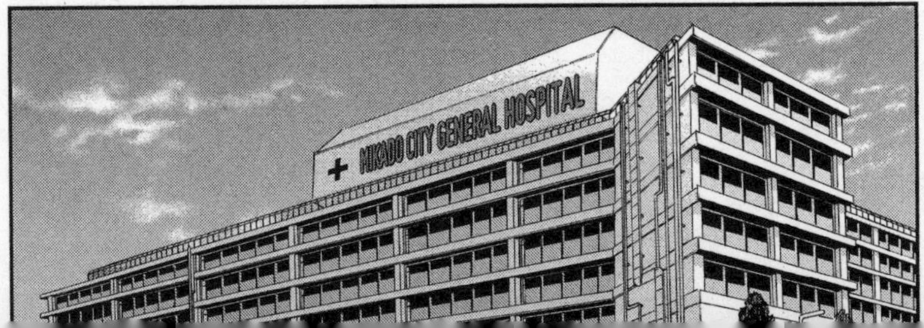
MIKADO CITY GENERAL HOSPITAL

Heyyy, Osamuuu.
WOBBLE
WOBBLE
Thank goodness ya regained conscious-ness...

USAMI ?!
WHAT'S WRONG?!

IMMA BIT SWEEP DEPRIVED ...
OH...

YOU JUST WOKE UP...
...SO I'LL GET TO THE POINT.

JUST TO INFORM YOU, WHILE YOU WERE SLEEPING, THEY GAVE OUT DISTINGUISHED SERVICE AWARDS.
OH, OKAY...

THERE ARE SPECIAL, OUTSTANDING AND EXCELLENT AWARDS BASED ON ACHIEVEMENTS...
THEY'RE BASICALLY BONUSES FOR PEOPLE WHO DID A GOOD JOB.
LET'S START WITH SPECIAL.

Special Distinguished Service

Reward: 1,500,000 yen [$15,000] + 1,500 points

Shuji Miwa
A-Rank #7
Miwa Squad

Intercepted and fought two humanoid Neighbors (Black Triggers) in front of HQ, forcing the enemy to withdraw.

Rabits defeated: 1

Yuma Kuga
Tamakoma Branch
Defeated a humanoid Neighbor (Black Trigger). Provided cover fire in the battle in front of HQ, contributing to the enemy's withdrawal.
Rabits defeated: 3
*Includes Replica's (Black Rabit) services

KUGA GOT THE SPECIAL DISTINGUISHED SERVICE AWARD?!

HEH HEH.
NEXT ARE THE OUTSTANDING DISTINGUISHED SERVICE AWARDS...

Osamu Mikumo
Tamakoma Branch
Supported the evacuation of C-Rank trainees from southwestern area to HQ. Attacked the Neighbor ship and forced them to withdraw.
Rabits defeated: 3
Outstanding Distinguished Service
Reward 800,000 yen [$8,000] + 800 points

WHO, ME?!
YOU TOTALLY DESERVE IT.
YOU WERE CRUCIAL IN DRIVING THE ENEMY BACK.

Haruaki Azuma
B-Rank #6
Azuma Squad

Took command of the battle against the humanoid Neighbors, contributing to their defeat. Rushed to the southern area to minimize damage to the city.

Kohei Izumi
A-Rank #1
Tachikawa Squad

Yosuke Yoneya
A-Rank #7
Miwa Squad

Shun Midorikawa
A-Rank #4
Kusakabe Squad

The main force in the battle against humanoid Neighbors, contributing to their defeat. Supported the evacuation of C-Rank trainees to HQ, preventing any loss of life.

Kazama Squad
A-Rank #3

Contributed to the defeat of the humanoid Neighbor (Black Trigger) who invaded HQ.

Rabits defeated: 4

Kirie Konami
Tamakoma Branch
Tamakoma-1

Supported the evacuation of C-Rank trainees from southwestern area to HQ. Pursued the Trion soldiers advancing into the southwest, preventing any loss of life.

Rabits defeated: 2

Arashiyama Squad
A-Rank #5

Stamped out enemy forces in the Forbidden Zone. Then provided backup support for Konami, protecting the citizens in the southwestern areas.

Rabits defeated: 5
*Includes the one Kitora defeated by herself

THEN THERE'S THE A-RANK SNIPER TEAM CONSISTING OF TOMA, NARASAKA AND SHOHEI.

B-RANK SUWA SQUAD.
KO FROM KURUMA SQUAD.

THE B-RANK SQUADS BUNDLED ALL TOGETHER: AZUMA, KURUMA, ARAFUNE, KAKIZAKI AND CHANO SQUADS.
DEFENSE ORGANIZATION
BORDER
MIKADO CITY
AND THAT'S IT!

So that's my report, at least.
I'm going home to sleep.
WOBBLE
WOBBLE
THANKS ...

SHOOP

HUH?

OSAMU.
HE'S HERE.
...?

HEY.

OSAMU.

!!

KUGA!

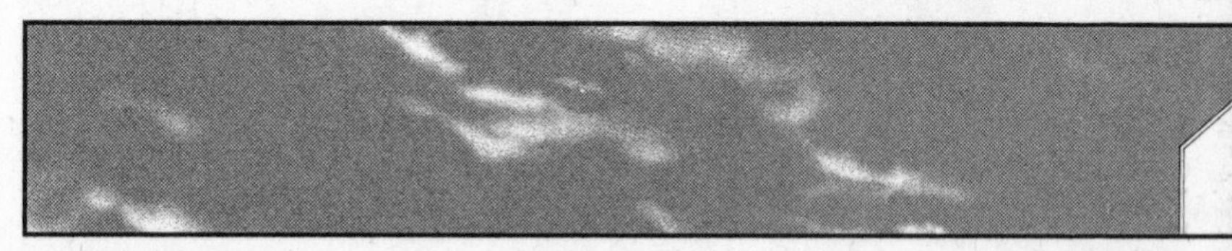

ABOUT REPLICA...
...!

AS SHIORI AND THE OTHERS SAY...
...IF REPLICA WERE REALLY DEAD...
...THIS MINI-REPLICA WOULD'VE DISAP-PEARED TOO.

SO AS LONG AS THIS IS AROUND...
...HE'S NOT DEAD YET.

SHE'S BEEN INVESTIGATING IT FOR DAYS NOW.
SO IT HAS TO BE RIGHT.

REPLICA IS STILL ALIVE.
I'LL SEE HIM AGAIN IF WE MAKE IT TO AFTOKRATOR.

NOW WE HAVE MORE REASON TO MAKE A-RANK.

...!
KUGA...

HE'S SAYING THIS...
...SO I WON'T FEEL BAD.

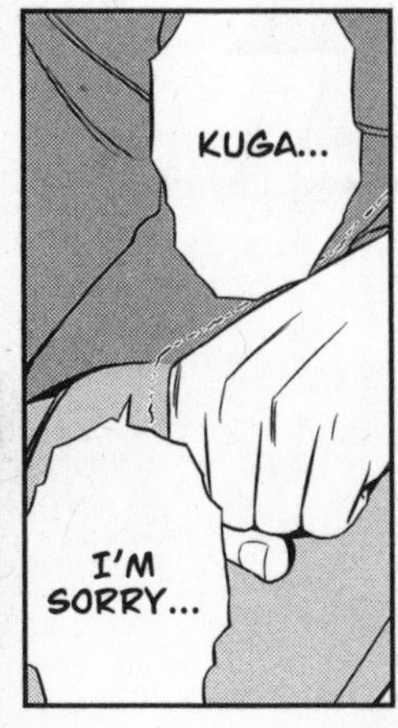
KUGA...
I'M SORRY...

IT'S MY FAULT...

I WASN'T STRONG ENOUGH!
THIS IS GOODBYE.
TAKE CARE OF YUMA.
AND NOW REPLICA IS GONE!

THAT'S NOT TRUE.

I TOLD REPLICA...
HE'S A DECOY TOO.
PROTECT CHIKA AND OSAMU.
...TO PROTECT YOU AND CHIKA.

AND HE DID ABSOLUTELY WHAT I ASKED.

YOU DON'T HAVE TO APOLOGIZE.

YOU SHOULD *PRAISE* REPLICA...
HE DID IT EVEN AFTER HE GOT CHOPPED IN HALF.

I WOULDN'T EXPECT ANYTHING LESS FROM MY PARTNER.

THERE YOU ARE.

MIKUMO.

CAN YOU COME TAKE A WALK WITH ME?

I'VE RECEIVED PERMISSION FROM YOUR DOCTORS.

This was an illustration I drew for the all-hands cover for the combined issue, where everyone dressed up as kabuki actors. The chronic pain in my neck was acting up again, so I went on hiatus that week and didn't get to use it. I felt bad for Yuma, so I'll put this here. My manager made it into a stamp for some reason. "Why the 3 yen stamp?" It's because of his 3-shaped mouth.

OSAMU ...?

YUMA!

Chapter 84 Osamu Mikumo: Part 10

HE'S BEEN INJURED.
HE CAN'T GO OUT YET...
I'VE RECEIVED PERMISSION FROM HIS DOCTORS.

IF YOU'RE WORRIED, I CAN GET MY CAR.
AS HIS SISTER, YOU CAN COME WITH US...

MOTHER.

..
HUH ...?

GENERAL HOSPITAL
YOUR... MOTHER ...?
MOTHER.

BORDER PRESS CONFERENCE
1 P.M.

A PRESS CONFERENCE?
THE PUBLIC WANTS TO KNOW WHAT HAPPENED DURING THE BATTLE.
PTAM

THAT CONCLUDES THE REPORT.
THE FACT THAT THERE WERE VICTIMS INSIDE BORDER...
...BRINGS INTO QUESTION BORDER'S DEFENSIVE CAPACITY.
WHAT DO YOU HAVE TO SAY ABOUT THAT?

THERE IS MORE DETAILED DATA IN YOUR HANDOUT.

WE'LL NOW ANSWER ANY QUESTIONS YOU MAY HAVE.

FIRST ...
WE OFFER OUR DEEPEST CONDO-LENCES...
...TO THE FAMILIES OF THE SIX STAFF MEMBERS.

THEY WERE TALENTED PEOPLE.
ALONG WITH THE 32 MISSING TRAINEES...
...IT IS A HUGE LOSS THAT WE REGRET.

...?!
GASP

PLEASE LOOK AGAIN AT YOUR HANDOUT.
THE SCALE OF THIS ATTACK...
...WAS ABOUT EIGHT TIMES THAT OF THE FIRST NEIGHBOR ATTACK FOUR AND A HALF YEARS AGO.

AT THE TIME, MORE THAN 1,200 DIED.
AND MORE THAN 400 PEOPLE WENT MISSING.
EIGHT TIMES AS MANY NEIGHBORS INVADED MIKADO CITY IN THIS RECENT ATTACK.

SO ONCE THE SCALE OF THE BATTLE IS LARGE ENOUGH...
...YOU'RE SAYING THAT THE LIVES OF 40 PEOPLE ARE A MARGIN OF ERROR?
I PERSONALLY KNOW SOMEONE WHOSE SON IS ONE OF THE MISSING.
WOULD YOU SAY THE SAME TO HIS PARENTS?

THE 32 MISSING TRAINEES...
...WERE LEADING THE EVACUATION CLOSE TO THE BATTLE-FRONT.

THEY CHOSE TO STAY EVEN THOUGH IT MEANT RISKING THEIR OWN SAFETY.
WE FEEL THAT IS WHAT LED TO ZERO CIVILIAN DEATHS.

WE CANNOT DISREGARD THEIR ENDEAVOR.
WE WERE ABLE TO PROTECT THE CIVILIANS BECAUSE OF THEIR SACRIFICE.

COULDN'T YOU HAVE AVOIDED THAT SACRIFICE?

WE KNOW BORDER HAS EMERGENCY ESCAPE TRIGGERS.
WHY DON'T YOU GIVE THEM TO THE TRAINEES TOO?

BECAUSE WE DON'T HAVE ENOUGH TRIGGERS!
WE'D EQUIP EVERYONE IN BORDER IF WE COULD!

TO MAKE EVEN ONE EMERGENCY ESCAPE TRIGGER...
...WE NEED MONEY, MATERIALS AND MAN-POWER!
DO YOU THINK THOSE THINGS GROW ON TREES?!
THINK BEFORE YOU ASK QUESTIONS!
...
SHP
IF THE TRAINEES WERE TARGETED THIS TIME...
...IS IT POSSIBLE THAT THE NEIGHBORS KNEW...
...THAT TRAINEES ARE UNABLE TO ESCAPE IN AN EMERGENCY?

THE TRAINEES ARE ONLY ALLOWED TO USE THEIR TRIGGERS INSIDE THE BASE...
...SO IT SHOULDN'T BE POSSIBLE FOR NEIGHBORS TO FIND OUT.

LAST MONTH...

...A LOCAL PUBLIC JUNIOR HIGH WAS ATTACKED BY A NEIGHBOR.

THERE ARE EYE-WITNESS ACCOUNTS...

...OF A TRAINEE AT THE SCENE USING A TRIGGER TO FIGHT.

...!

BUZZ

BUZZ

IS IT POSSIBLE THAT INFORMATION LEAKED TO NEIGHBORS THEN?

EVEN THOUGH IT MAY NOT HAVE BEARING IN THIS CASE...
...PLEASE CONSIDER THAT THIS AGENT BROKE THE RULES TO PROTECT HIS CLASSMATES.
IN FACT, MANY STUDENTS WERE SAVED...

HERE WE GO.

THAT REPORTER...
...WAS A PLANT BY MR. NETSUKI.

WHAT ?!

HIS JOB...
...IS TO DIVERT THE PRESS'S WRATH FROM ALL OF BORDER TO ONE AGENT.

WE DON'T KNOW WHAT THEY'D WRITE ABOUT IF WE GAVE THEM NOTHING.
SO WE'RE OFFERING THEM SOMETHING EASY TO UNDERSTAND.

SO THEY'RE GOING TO BLAME EVERYTHING ON OSAMU.
THROB
THROB
OSAMU... ARE YOU OKAY?
...

MR. KARASAWA...
DID YOU BRING ME HERE TO SHOW ME THIS?

YES.
WE KNEW THIS WAS GOING TO HAPPEN.
I THOUGHT YOU MIGHT WANT TO KNOW.

WHAT NOW, OSAMU?
WANT ME TO KICK THAT GUY'S BUTT?

WE CAN'T DO ANYTHING...

IF WHAT HE SAID IS TRUE...
...THEN THIS ***IS*** MY FAULT.

...

OSAMU...

YOU MAKE UP SOME STUPID LIES.

SIGH

BORDER
MIKADO CITY
IF THE SAME THING HAPPENED AGAIN...
WHAT WOULD YOU DO?

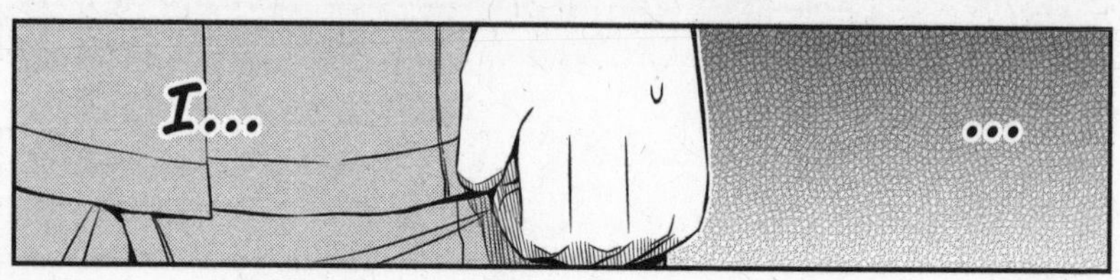
...
I...

KUGA...
SORRY.

I HAVE TO DO THIS.

SURE.
GO AHEAD.

...
YOU MAKE A GOOD TEAM.

MR. KARASAWA, WHY...
...ARE YOU ON OSAMU'S SIDE?

IT'S NOT THAT I'M ON HIS SIDE...

IF I SAW PEOPLE UNDER ATTACK...
...I THINK I'D STILL RESCUE THEM.

IT'S JUST THAT...

A HERO SHOULD BE GIVEN...

...A CHANCE TO FIGHT BACK, RIGHT?

Border Senior Officers

Masamune Kido
HQ Commander

■42 years old
■Born Sept. 1

■Lupus, Blood type O
■Height: 5'10"
■Likes: Family, old movies, black coffee

Motokichi Kinuta
HQ R&D Director

■48 years old
■Born July 14

■Gladius, Blood type B
■Height: 5'3"
■Likes: Family, work, instant noodles, taking walks

Eizo Netsuki
PR Director

■39 years old
■Born June 2

■Lepus, Blood type A
■Height: 5'6"
■Likes: Tea, horses, gardening, collecting Border merchandise

Katsumi Karasawa
HQ Business Director

■33 years old
■Born May 17

■Felis, Blood type B
■Height: 5'10"
■Likes: Cigarettes, rugby, spicy cod roe, kettle pilaf

TMP

Chapter 84
Osamu Mikumo: Part 11

HE LOOKS INJURED...
BZZ
WHO'S THAT...?
MIKUMO!
SKRUT
HEY, HEY.

MY NAME IS OSAMU MIKUMO.
I'M THE TRAINEE...
...WHO USED A TRIGGER AT SCHOOL LAST MONTH.
IF YOU HAVE ANY QUESTIONS...
...I'LL ANSWER THEM DIRECTLY.
THAT KID?
THEN HE'S THE ONE TO BLAME...
PLEASE REFRAIN FROM ACCUSING OUR AGENTS BASED PURELY ON CONJECTURE.

HE'S CURRENTLY AN AGENT.
AS FOR THE REGULATION VIOLATION IN QUESTION...
...IT WAS DEALT WITH MORE THAN A MONTH AGO! THAT MATTER IS CLOSED.

YES, THAT'S RIGHT.
GANGING UP ON A **CHILD** IS SO...

HE SAID HE WANTS TO TALK!
SO LET HIM!
YEAH, YEAH!

OSAMU ...
ARE YOU SURE ABOUT THIS?
I'M VERY SURE.

BUT...
...I MIGHT END UP CAUSING PROBLEMS FOR BORDER.

DON'T WORRY ABOUT IT.
DO WHAT YOU WANT.

SINCE AN ABNORMAL GATE OPENED AT SCHOOL...

...IT MEANS A RAD MUST'VE BEEN CLOSE BY AT THE TIME.

THINKING BACK...

...THAT POSSIBILITY DOES EXIST.

...!!

BRUTALLY HONEST, AS ALWAYS.

DON'T YOU UNDER-STAND THE SERIOUS-NESS OF THIS MATTER ?!
WE'VE LOST 32 PEOPLE!

"THINKING BACK," YOU SAY?!
WE DESERVE A BETTER EXPLANA-TION!
...

I'M NOT TRYING TO EXPLAIN THINGS AWAY.

EVEN IF I HAD KNOWN THE INFORMATION MIGHT LEAK...
...I THINK I WOULD'VE STILL USED THE TRIGGER.
THAT'S HOW BAD THE SITUATION WAS.

EVEN IF THAT MEANT CREATING FURTHER VICTIMS?!
YES.
EVEN IF THERE WAS A POSSIBILITY OF FUTURE CASUALTIES...
...THAT WOULDN'T BE A REASON TO ABANDON PEOPLE WHO NEEDED HELP RIGHT THEN.

I'M NOT A HERO.
I CAN'T DO THE KIND OF THING WHERE EVERYONE IS PLEASED WITH THE RESULT.
I CAN ONLY DO WHAT I THINK I SHOULD DO...
...IN A WAY I WON'T REGRET LATER.
WE'RE SUPPOSED TO OVERLOOK YOUR MISTAKES BECAUSE YOU'RE A NOVICE?!
YOU'RE NOT SORRY AT ALL!
WHAT ABOUT THE VICTIMS AND THEIR FAMILIES?!
HAVE YOU NO SENSE OF GUILT?!

THOSE REPORTERS...
...NEED TO BE BEATEN WITH A STICK.

CAN'T YOU SHOW SOME HUMILITY?
IT SOUNDS LIKE YOU'RE TRYING TO JUSTIFY YOURSELF.

OUR QUESTION IS...
...HOW ARE YOU GOING TO MAKE UP...
...FOR THE 32 LIVES LOST BECAUSE OF YOU?

HOW ARE YOU GOING TO TAKE RESPONSI-BILITY?
I'LL GET THEM BACK.

YOUR FAMILY MEMBERS WHO WERE TAKEN BY NEIGHBORS...
YOUR FRIENDS...
WE'LL GO GET THEM BACK.
YOU DON'T HAVE TO TELL ME ABOUT TAKING RESPONSIBILITY.
IT'S THE OBVIOUS THING TO DO.
UH...
...?!
GET THEM BACK?
WHAT DOES HE MEAN?
GOING TO THE NEIGHBOR WORLD?!
MR MR
MRMR

BUT...

THE TIDE IS TURNING.

LIKE HE SAID...

...WE AT BORDER ARE PROCEEDING...

...WITH PLANS FOR A MISSION TO RECOVER THE ABDUCTED PEOPLE.

IN FACT...
...WE'VE SUCCEEDED IN TRIAL UNMANNED ROUND TRIPS TO THE NEIGHBOR WORLD.
...?!

COM-MANDER KIDO!

OH, I GET IT.
YOU'RE GOING TO PRETEND YOU'RE JUST STARTING TO GO.

PST
SENDING AGENTS TO THE NEIGHBOR WORLD...?
PST
PST
ISN'T THAT DANGER-OUS?
THERE COULD BE FURTHER VICTIMS JUST TO SAVE THESE 32...

AH YES, YOU'RE OF THE OPINION...
...THAT WE SHOULD ABANDON JUST THOSE 32 AND MOVE ON.

URK
...

THIS RECOVERY MISSION ISN'T JUST ABOUT THE 32 PEOPLE KIDNAPPED THIS TIME...

...BUT THE MORE THAN 400 CITIZENS WHO WENT MISSING IN THE VERY FIRST ATTACK.

IT WILL BE BORDER'S MOST SIGNIFICANT LONG-TERM PROJECT TO DATE.

WE ARE IN NEED OF MORE MANPOWER.

FRONT-LINE COMBAT-ANTS...

...THE STAFF SUP-PORTING THEM...

...AND THIS CITY ITSELF, WHICH SUPPORTS OUR ORGANIZATION.

WE EXPECT YOUR UNDER-STANDING AND PARTICIPA-TION...

...IN CONSIDERATION OF THE RECOVERY MISSION, IN ADDITION TO THE USUAL DEFENSE ACTIVITIES.

THAT IS ALL I HAVE TO SAY.

HOW ARE YOU GOING TO DECIDE THE PERSONNEL FOR THE RECOVERY MISSION?

IS MIKUMO INCLUDED AMONG THE MEMBERS?

WE WILL ASK FOR VOLUNTEERS AND SELECT FROM THEM.
A-Rank [elite] 30 people
B-Rank [main force]
THEY WILL BE A-RANK OR ABOVE...
...AND A SELECTION EXAM WILL BE CARRIED OUT.
WHETHER HE WILL TAKE PART IN THE MISSION...
...WILL PURELY DEPEND ON HIS ABILITY TO MEET THE CRITERIA.
YES.
I KNOW.
YOU MAY STEP DOWN NOW...
YOUR FIRST DUTY IS TO HEAL.
YES, SIR.
A RECOVERY PLAN TO BRING PEOPLE BACK...!
YADDA
A MISSION TO THE NEIGHBOR WORLD...?
YADDA
THIS'LL BE A HUGE STORY!

YADDA
YADDA

PTAM

PHEW ...

HEY, OSAMU.

NICE SPEECH.
SPEECH ...?

...
YOU ALMOST GOT YOURSELF KILLED.
YOU'RE GOING TO KEEP DOING THIS?

...!
MOM...

WHEN YOU BROUGHT THE PAPERWORK TO ENLIST SIX MONTHS AGO...
DO YOU REMEMBER THAT I WAS TOTALLY AGAINST IT?

WHEN I HEARD YOU GOT SERIOUSLY INJURED...
...MY FIRST THOUGHT WAS, "I TOLD YOU SO."
...

BUT IT'S STRANGE...
ALL THOSE PEOPLE CAME TO VISIT YOU, BUT...
...EVEN AFTER SEEING YOU MOTIONLESS ON THE BED...
...NONE OF THEM SUGGESTED THAT YOU SHOULD QUIT BORDER.

HUH?
I WONDERED WHY, BUT...
...I UNDERSTAND A BIT BETTER NOW.

EVER SINCE YOU JOINED BORDER...
...YOU LOOK LIKE YOU'VE FOUND WHAT YOU WANT TO DO.

YOU SHOULD DO WHAT YOU BELIEVE YOU MUST...
IT'S YOUR LIFE, AFTER ALL.
JUST LET ME KNOW WHEN YOU GET SICK OF IT.
I'LL DRAG YOU BACK IF I HAVE TO ROPE YOU AROUND THE NECK.

THANKS...
MOM.

NOW THAT YOU'VE OPENED YOUR BIG MOUTH, WE GOTTA STEP IT UP.
GEEZ, OSAMU.

IT'S WHAT WE WERE GOING TO DO ANYWAY.
TOK
WE'LL MAKE A-RANK AS FAST AS WE CAN.

LET'S DO THIS.
PARTNER.

SURE.
YOU CAN COUNT ON ME.

I'M SO GLAD...
OSAMU... YUMA...

HE'S BACK.

YOU REALLY ARE A HERO.

Mikumo Squad (Tamakoma-2)

Border B-Rank Wars

B-RANK

■001 NINOMIYA ■002 KAGEURA
■003 IKOMA ■004 YUBA
■005 OJI ■006 AZUMA
■007 KATORI

■008 SUZUNARI-1 (KURUMA)
■009 URUSHIMA ■010 SUWA
■011 ARAFUNE ■012 NASU
■013 KAKIZAKI ■014 HAYAKAWA

■015 MATSUSHIRO ■016 YOSHIZATO
■017 MAMIYA ■018 EBINA
■019 CHANO ■020 TOKIWA
■021 TAMAKOMA-2 (MIKUMO)

Start

The Way They Were: Part 3

Such Nostalgia

Kako [early version]

It's weird to talk about differences for a character who hasn't really appeared that much, but she looks more down-to-earth in this version. She was going to be Tachikawa's childhood friend, but that's now Tsukimi. She still looks confident. I really like this hairstyle, so I'll save it for someone else.

Satori [early version]

This is from back when he was supposed to be popular with girls. How did he turn out the way he is now? The good looks and forehead went to Yoneya and his genius went to Izumi and then only his stupidity remained. I prefer him as he is now.

Kuroe [early version]

She hasn't appeared that much either, but she looks meaner here than she does now. I think she was supposed to be like a rabid dog-type character who would do anything Kako says. Just like how Midorikawa beat up Osamu. What happened to her?

Chapter 86 Tamakoma-2

YUMA, THAT MEANS LOSING YOUR BONUS POINTS...
...SO YOU'LL HAVE TO EARN YOUR WAY UP TO B-RANK.
THAT'S FINE.
NOT A PROBLEM.
OSAMU, ARE YOU OKAY GIVING YOURS UP TOO?
YES.
I WAS BASICALLY FIGHTING WITH HER TRION ANYWAY...
GOOD.
RANK WARS START AT THE BEGINNING OF FEBRUARY.
Rank Wars | Break
Feb, March, April | May
June, July, August | Sept
Oct, Nov, Dec | January
THAT'S WHEN YOU'LL UNVEIL THE B-RANK TAMAKOMA-2 SQUAD.
Chapter 86 Tamakoma-2

THE UNIFORMS DIDN'T MAKE IT IN TIME...

OH WELL.
WE'LL SAVE IT FOR NEXT WEEK WHEN WE CAN ALL WEAR THEM.
YEAH.

I'LL BE WATCHING FROM THE STANDS TODAY.
I'M COUNTING ON YOU TWO.

GOTCHA.
SEE YOU LATER!

WHIRR

TAK
MIKUMO...

YES.
I'LL TAKE PART IN THE RANK WARS NEXT WEEK.
I SEE...
ABOUT THE PRESS CONFERENCE...
NOW THAT YOU'RE HEALED...
...IS THERE ANYTHING YOU'D LIKE TO SAY ABOUT IT?
NO.
NOTHING.
I UNDERSTAND IT WAS **ANOTHER WAY TO FIGHT**.
BUT YOU SHOULD KNOW...

IF YOU TRY THE SAME KIND OF THING ON KUGA OR CHIKA...
...I WILL NEVER FORGIVE YOU.

I SEE...
I'LL REMEMBER THAT.

LET ME SAY ONE THING.

DIREC-TORS...
...RINDO AND SHINODA WERE NOT INVOLVED.

IF THEY HAD KNOWN, THEY WOULDN'T HAVE ALLOWED IT TO HAPPEN.

GOOD LUCK. WORK HARD...
...TO FULFILL YOUR GOALS.

■011 ARAFUNE ■012 NASU
■013 KAKIZAKI ■014 HAYAKAWA

■015 MATSUSHIRO ■016 YOSHIZATO
■017 MAMIYA ■018 EBINA
■019 CHANO ■020 TOKIWA
■021 TAMAKOMA-2 (MIKUMO)

GOOD EVENING, BORDER FOLKS!

OPERATOR FOR EBINA SQUAD SAKURAKO TAKETOMI HERE!

SAKURAKO TAKETOMI (15)
OPERATOR
EBINA SQUAD
B-RANK #18

...THE AGENTS HAVE BEEN SENT IN...

BEGIN TRANSMISSION

- 01 6 YOSHIZATO SQUAD
- 01 7 MAMIYA SQUAD
- 021 TAMAKOMA-2 (MIKUMO SQU

...WHILE WE WERE TALKING.

B-RANK

■001 NINOMIYA

■003 IKOMA

■005 OJI

■007 KATORI

■008 SUZUNARI-1

■009 URUSHIMA

B-RANK SQUADS ARE DIVIDED INTO THREE GROUPS: TOP, MIDDLE AND BOTTOM.

THERE ARE 21 TEAMS RIGHT NOW, SO SEVEN IN EACH.

THANK YOU, SATORI!
IF I MAY ADD ONE THING...

THE TOP TEAMS FROM LAST SEASON...
...GET INITIAL BONUS POINTS ACCORDING TO THEIR PREVIOUS PLACING.
PREVIOUS PLACING
INITIAL BONUS
1ST 15PT
2ND 14PT
3RD 13PT
4TH 12PT
5TH
6TH
7TH
8TH
9TH
10TH 6PT
11TH 5PT
4PT
SO THEY GET AN ADVANTAGE!
YEAH, THAT!

OKAY...
YOSHIZATO, MAMIYA, TAMAKOMA-2.
ALL SQUADS IN PLACE!
THE BATTLE HAS ALREADY BEGUN!

ARE TAMA-KOMA-2 GRADE SCHOOL-ERS?
HOW'D THEY GET TO B-RANK?
ACTUALLY, I HEAR THEY'RE SOMETHING SPECIAL.

YOUR PEOPLE HAVE A NUMBERS DISADVAN-TAGE...
...AGAINST YOSHIZATO AND MAMIYA SQUADS.
WHAT DO YOU SAY TO THAT, CAPTAIN MIKUMO?

ZWING
?!

SLASH
!!

KRAK

?!
HUH ?!
THAT WAS FAST!!
YOSHIZATO SQUAD WAS ANNIHILATED ALREADY?!
THOSE WERE NOT MERE B-RANK MOVES...
...FROM AGENT KUGA OF TAMAKOMA-2!
YOSHIZATO SQUAD BAILED OUT!
WHAT WILL MAMIYA SQUAD DO?!
HE BEAT MIDORIKAWA.
WE SHOULDN'T GO HEAD-TO-HEAD WITH HIM.
AAAND... THEY'RE NOT MOVING!
THEY WON'T MOVE AWAY FROM THE BUILDING!

EVERYONE ON MAMIYA SQUAD IS A SHOOTER!

THEIR SIMULTANEOUS FULL-ON ATTACK, "HOUND STORM," WILL BE SUPER POWERFUL IF IT CONNECTS!

OOH, THIS MIGHT BE TRICKY!

WE'LL SEE!

CHIKA?

CAN YOU SHOOT THAT BUILDING?

BORDER

SHIORI USAMI (17)
OPERATOR
TAMAKOMA-1,2

YES!
BLAM

WHOA ?!
DWUH ?!

BOO
THERE IT IS!!
SHK
EEN

KRAK
LIMIT EXCEEDED.
BAIL OUT.
FOOM

WHA—
WHAT A SHOCKING ENDING!!
SNIPER AGENT AMATORI DEMOLISHED THE WHOLE BUILDING WITH HER IBIS!!
IS SHE ALLOWED TO BE THAT POWERFUL?!

ONCE YOU ADD THE SURVIVAL BONUS, THAT'S EIGHT POINTS ALL AT ONCE!

WOW!

THIS TEAM IS TOUGH!!

...ARAFUNE SQUAD...
...WHO ARE CURRENTLY IN 10TH PLACE!
AND...
SUWA SQUAD, IN EIGHTH PLACE!
WE'LL BE WATCHING THESE NEW B-RANK STARS...
...AS THEY BATTLE AGAIN NEXT TIME. DON'T MISS IT!

Border Senior Officers

Masafumi Shinoda
HQ Director

■33 years old
■Born Oct. 16

■Falcata,
Blood type A
■Height: 5'11"
■Likes: Training, rolled omelet, soy sauce, ramen, motorbikes

Kyoko Sawamura
HQ Assistant Director

■25 years old
■Born July 22

■Gladius,
Blood type A
■Height: 5'5"
■Likes: Supporting the Director, exercise, roasted chestnuts

Takumi Rindo
Tamakoma Branch Director

■34 years old
■Born Nov. 2

■Chronos,
Blood type AB
■Height: 5'10"
■Likes: Cigarettes, ramen with salt-based soup, animals, fishing (though he's bad at it)

Chapter 87 Tamakoma-2: Part 2

HE'S NOT BACK UP TO FULL SPEED YET.
THE PRESS CONFERENCE SET BACK HIS RECOVERY.
HA HA.
SORRY ABOUT THAT.

YOTARO AND KONAMI WERE SO MAD.
MOSTLY AT MR. NETSUKI AND THE REPORTERS.
IS THAT SO.

WHY DID YOU TAKE FOUR-EYES THERE?
IT FELT LIKE A MISUSE OF RESOURCES.

THEY ONLY WANTED SOMEONE TO BLAME.
WASTING MIKUMO AS A SCAPEGOAT...
...DIDN'T SIT RIGHT WITH ME.

YOU THINK VERY HIGHLY OF HIM.
PRETTY MUCH.
RIGHT AFTER THE INVASION...
...26 PEOPLE QUIT BORDER.

BUT SINCE THAT PRESS CONFERENCE...
...FIVE TIMES THAT NUMBER HAVE APPLIED.
MORE COMPANIES WANT TO BE SPONSORS.

ARE YOU SAYING THAT'S ALL THANKS TO FOUR-EYES?
NOT DIRECTLY.
THE CONCEPT OF AN EXPEDITION TO THE NEIGHBOR WORLD HAS SPARKED THEIR IMAGINATIONS.

THAT'S ALL THE MEDIA IS TALKING ABOUT.
NHN
PRESS RELEASE
NEW DEFENSE STRATEGY
FIRST AWAY MISSION

BUT...
...HE'S THE ONE WHO PUSHED US IN THAT DIRECTION.
HE CARRIES RISK, SURE.
BUT SOME PEOPLE VALUE THAT KIND OF PERSON.

I'M ONE OF THEM.
JIN.

DON'T STAY DEPRESSED TOO LONG.
PAT
YOU SHOULD GO CHEER ON YOUR JUNIORS.

MIKUMO HAS A TOUGH ROAD AHEAD OF HIM.
...

I'M NOT QUICK TO MOVE ON LIKE YOU ARE, MR. KARASAWA.
I USED TO PLAY RUGBY, AFTER ALL.
HOW IS THAT RELATED...?

PEOPLE!

CONGRA-CHOO-LATIONS ON YOUR FIRST VICTORY!

UNLIKE THE BOTTOM GROUP YOU GUYS PUMMELED...
...THE MIDDLE B-RANK GROUP YOU'LL FIGHT ON WEDNESDAY IS KIND OF SO-SO.
EACH SQUAD HAS A UNIQUE STRATEGY, AND THEY HAVE THEIR ACT TOGETHER.

"KIND OF SO-SO"?
HM.
AND THE TOP GROUP?

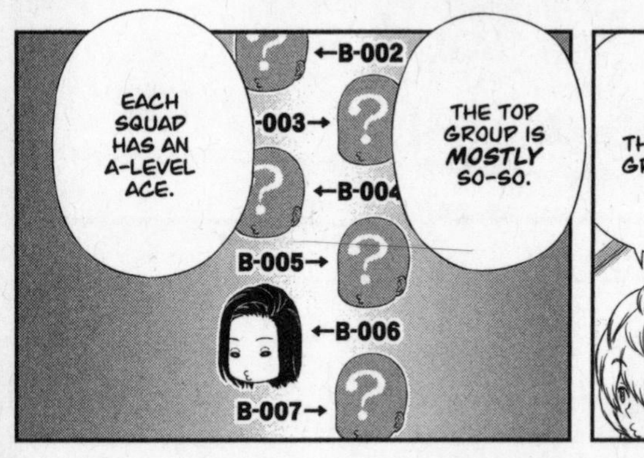
THE TOP GROUP IS *MOSTLY* SO-SO.
EACH SQUAD HAS AN A-LEVEL ACE.
←B-002
-003→
←B-004
B-005→
←B-006
B-007→

SOME OF THEM ACTUALLY USED TO BE A-RANK.
THEY'RE BASICALLY A-RANK RESERVES.
WHAT ABOUT A-RANK ...?

A-RANK IS...
SUPER SO-SO.
IS "SO-SO" THE ONLY DESIGNATION?
KONAMI SURE HATES TO LOSE...

SERIOUSLY, YOU SHOULDN'T UNDERESTIMATE THE MIDDLE B-RANK SQUADS.

THEY HAVE A LOT MORE EXPERIENCE ...
...THAN CHIKA OR OSAMU.

WE'RE UP AGAINST SUWA AND ARAFUNE SQUADS NEXT.
WHAT ARE THEY LIKE?

SUWA IS...
KYOSUKE.

DON'T TELL THEM EVERYTHING.
THEY CAN DO THE RESEARCH.
REIJI...

DATA ON PAST RANK WARS IS IN THE STRATEGY ROOM.

LOOK IT OVER BEFORE USAMI GETS HERE.
OKAY!
ROGER.

YOU DON'T EVEN KNOW HOW TO GO THROUGH THE DATA.
I'LL TEACH YOU!
ME TOO.
AS YOUR SENIOR.

AREN'T YOU BEING A LITTLE HARSH...?
COMING UP WITH COUNTER-MEASURES IS PART OF THE TRAINING.

THEIR BATTLE...
...HAS ALREADY BEGUN.
BORDER

Border HQ
Lounge

ISN'T TAMAKOMA-2 THE ONE...
...WITH THAT ALBINO SHRIMP?
KOTARO SUWA (21)
GUNNER
SUWA SQUAD
B-RANK #8 (FOR NOW)
B-008

AND FOUR-EYES, WHOSE MOCK BATTLE WITH KAZAMA ENDED IN A DRAW.
DAICHI TSUTSUMI (20)
GUNNER

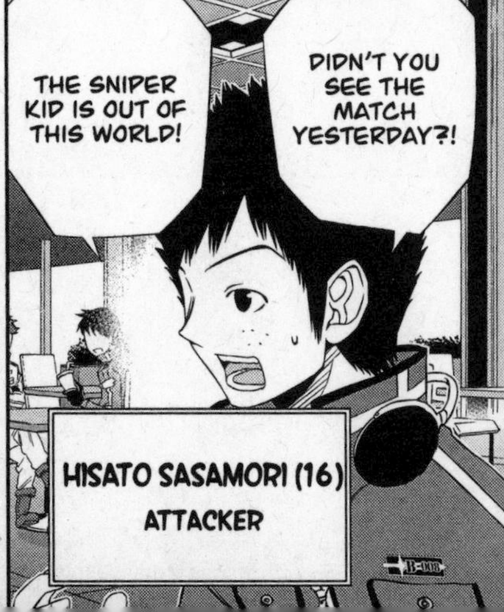
DIDN'T YOU SEE THE MATCH YESTERDAY?!
THE SNIPER KID IS OUT OF THIS WORLD!
HISATO SASAMORI (16)
ATTACKER

NEVER HEARD OF ANY OF 'EM!
RUI OSANO (17)
OPERATOR

THAT MIGHT AS WELL BE A CANNON !!

THE WHITE-HAIRED KID MOVES WELL.

THEY'RE BOTH PUNY.

THE SNIPER IS REIJI'S PUPIL.

WHAT ?!

HOW DOES PHYSICS WORK IN THAT RELATIONSHIP ?!
WHAT'S THAT BEEFCAKE GORILLA THINKING?!

REIJI IS A SMART BEEFCAKE.
OSANO, THAT'S BESIDE THE POINT.

WITH REIJI AS HER MENTOR, SHE SHOULD HAVE THE BASICS DOWN.

THE WHITE-HAIRED KID BEAT MIDORIKAWA IN A SOLO MATCH.
I THINK BY 8-2.
8-2?!

HISATO, HOW WOULD YOU FARE WITH MIDORIKAWA IN A TEN-MATCH DUEL?
I GOT FOUR ONCE, BUT IT WAS A FLUKE.

ALL RIGHT, HISATO.
STOP THE SHRIMP FOR TWO SECONDS.
WE'LL BLOW THEM AWAY.
ISN'T THAT THE STRATEGY WHERE I GET BLOWN AWAY TOO?

Border HQ
Arafune Squad Strategy Room

OH MAN.
THAT POWER.
I SAW HER AT TRAINING.
SHE WAS USING AN EGRET THEN.

SHE'S THE ONE WHO BLEW A HOLE IN THE BASE.
TETSUJI ARAFUNE (18)
SNIPER
ARAFUNE SQUAD
B-RANK #10 (FOR NOW)

IS IT THE DAWN...
...OF A NEW ERA FOR SNIPERS?
ATSUSHI HOKARI (18)
SNIPER

IT WOULD SUCK IF SHE KEPT BLASTING AWAY AT THE GOOD SNIPING PERCHES.
YOSHITO HANZAKI (15)
SNIPER

NO CHANCE OF THAT.

SHE MAKES HER LOCATION OBVIOUS.
WE'D GET HER BEFORE THE SECOND SHOT.
THAT'S TRUE.

I FOUND DATA ON KUGA.
HE DID A SOLO MATCH WITH MIDORIKAWA.
I FOUND THE SAME DATA FOR MIKUMO, BUT HE LOST 10-0.
RIN KAGAMI (18)
OPERATOR

IS MIKUMO A SHOOTER?

NOT MUCH DATA ON HIM...

I SAW HIM.

AT THE PRESS CONFERENCE.

OH, THE GUY WITH GLASSES?

GATHER **ALL** THEIR DATA.

I'LL MEMORIZE THEIR HABITS.

THEN THE ONLY ISSUE WOULD BE...

...**WHERE** THEY'LL CHOOSE...

HOW'S IT GOING?
HI, SHIORI.
WE'RE LOOKING UP DATA ON OUR NEXT OPPONENTS.
ARE YOU?

SUWA SQUAD HAS TWO GUNNERS AND ONE ATTACKER.
THEIR TACTICAL FORMATION IS A TIGHT CLUSTER.

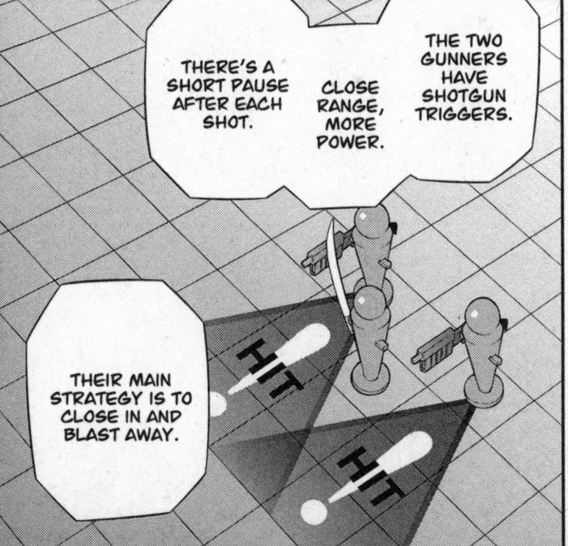

THE ATTACKER WORKS AS A SHIELD TO PROVIDE COVER FOR THEM.
BUT HE USES A CHAMELEON FOR SNEAK ATTACKS.
GUARD
IF WE TRY TO EXPAND OUR OWN SHIELDS TO BLOCK THE BULLETS...
...HE WILL COME IN, INVISIBLE, TO SLICE THEM.

YEAH, THAT PRETTY MUCH SUMS IT UP.
SO, WHAT ARE YOU GOING TO DO?

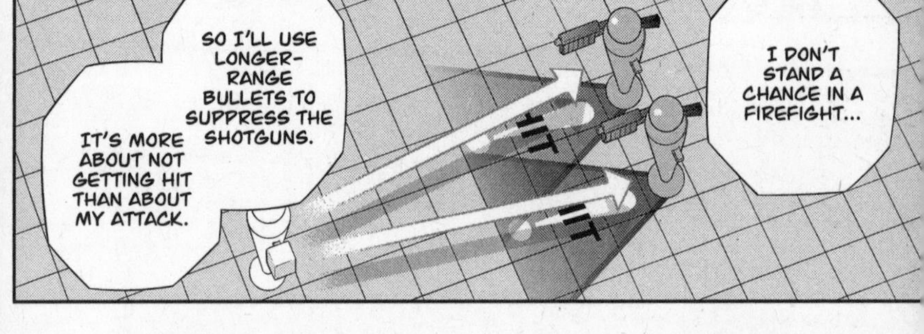

ALL THREE MEMBERS OF ARAFUNE SQUAD ARE SNIPERS.

THEY'RE THE TOTAL OPPOSITE OF SUWA SQUAD—THEIR FORMATION IS SPREAD WIDE.

SHOT

COVER

SHOT

SHOT

COVER

THEY UTILIZE THEIR RANGE AND TEAMWORK FOR BOTH DEFENSE AND OFFENSE.

THEY'LL BE TOUGH FOR US TO TOPPLE.

WE THOUGHT OF SHOOTING THE BUILDINGS OUT WITH CHIKA'S IBIS, BUT...
SHE'D GET DISCOVERED, SO NO-GO!
SHE'LL SHOOT ONLY AT THE CRITICAL MOMENT.
GOOD IDEA.

WE DIDN'T USE IT YESTERDAY...
...BUT THE LOWEST-RANKED TEAM...
...GETS TO PICK THE BATTLE STAGE.

TAMAKOMA-2 IS LOWEST IN THE NEXT MATCH...
...SO WE CAN PICK THE STAGE THAT'S BEST FOR US.
No. 8: Suwa Squad
No. 10: Arafune Squad
No. 12: Tamakoma-2

YEAH, THAT WOULD BE AN ADVANTAGE.
SO WE CAN USE THE TERRAIN TO BLOCK THEIR SNIPING!

OKAY.
THREE DAYS LEFT.
WE'LL PICK A STAGE AND COME UP WITH A PLAN!
ROGER!

Wednesday, February 5
B-Rank Wars Round 2
B-RANK
ROUND 2
MIDDLE GROUP (NIGHT)
008 SUWA SQUAD
010 ARAFUNE SQUAD
012 TAMAKOMA-2

Q&A From Jump Festa 2015

Tomo Muranaka (Yuma's voice)

Q: Can Replica eat food??

A: He can't get nutrition from it, but he can eat to test for poison. He could survive in the wild with no problems.

Yuki Kaji (Osamu's voice)

Q: Why don't Jin's sunglasses slip down?

A: They attach behind his head.

Nao Tamura (Chika's voice)

Q: Can Replica sleep?

A: He doesn't need sleep, but he has a sleep mode. He waits (sleeps) inside Yuma's ring when he isn't needed.

Yuichi Nakamura (Jin's voice)

Q: How powerful was Yugo Kuga (Yuma's dad) compared to current characters?

A: Probably the same as Director Shinoda. He was stronger than Mr. Shinoda four years ago, but Mr. Shinoda caught up by training every day.

■ At the Jump Festa 2015 stage event in December 2014, there was a fan event where the voice actors in the World Trigger anime asked me questions. I answered them before the event so I wasn't on the stage, but I heard the event went over well with the fans. A lot of letters requested that we print the Q&A from the event here.

HERE'S TO THE NEW SEASON OF B-RANK WARS!

THE SECOND NIGHT IS ABOUT TO BEGIN!

DOING THE PLAY-BY-PLAY AGAIN—I SOMEHOW FOUND TIME IN MY SCHEDULE...

IT'S ME! SAKURAKO TAKETOMI!

Chapter 88 Tamakoma-2: Part 3

IN THE BOOTH WITH ME ARE TWO PEOPLE WHO RECEIVED OUTSTANDING SERVICE AWARDS IN THE RECENT INVASION...

AZUMA'S DOING COMMENTARY!
LET'S GO WATCH.
TODAY'S TEAM TO WATCH...
...HAS GOT TO BE TAMAKOMA-2, WHO SCORED A PERFECT EIGHT POINTS IN THEIR PREVIOUS MATCH!

IN EVIDENCE OF THE ATTENTION THEY HAVE GOTTEN...

...WE SEE SOME OFF-DUTY A-RANK AGENTS IN THE STANDS!

SO, AZUMA.
YOU DON'T OFTEN SEE PEOPLE GETTING EIGHT POINTS IN ONE MATCH, DO YOU?
IT'S PRETTY AMAZING.

IT MEANS TAMAKOMA-2 ISN'T A REGULAR ROOKIE TEAM.
YUMA'S GOOD.
HE MADE B-RANK REALLY FAST.
MIDORIKAWA, I HEARD YOU FOUGHT SOLO AGAINST AGENT KUGA...
GEE, THANKS FOR BRINGING THAT UP.

I LOST, OKAY? 8-2!
IT WAS A TOTAL SLAUGHTER!

BUT WE PROMISED TO DUEL AGAIN.
I'LL WIN NEXT TIME!

WAIT, SHUN LOST?
8-2?
IT WAS A GOOD MATCH.

TAMA-KOMA-2'S OPPONENTS TODAY...
...ARE CLOSE-COMBAT SUWA SQUAD...
...AND LONG-RANGE ARAFUNE SQUAD.
TWO SQUADS WITH CLEAR-CUT FIGHTING STYLES!

SINCE TAMAKOMA-2 IS RANKED LOWEST, THEY GET TO PICK THE STAGE.
THEY'LL WANT TO GET THE TOPO-GRAPHICAL ADVANTAGE.

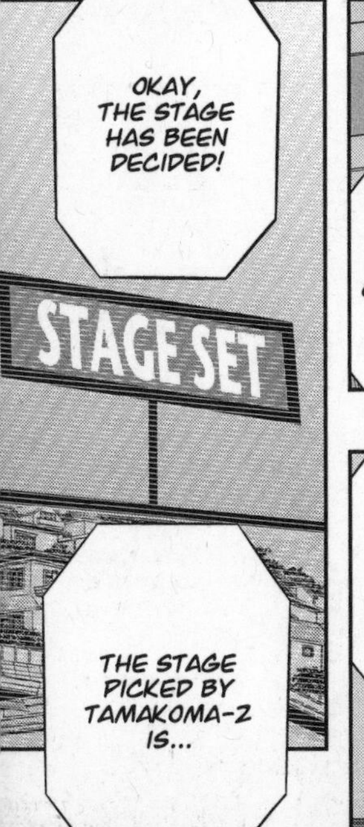
OKAY, THE STAGE HAS BEEN DECIDED!
STAGE SET
THE STAGE PICKED BY TAMAKOMA-2 IS...

■ CITYSCAPE C
CITYSCAPE C!
IT'S A HILLSIDE RESIDENTIAL AREA!

...?!

SEEMS LIKE...
...THIS SETTING IS GREAT FOR SNIPERS.
YES... IT IS.

THE HOUSES ARE BUILT INTO THE SLOPE.
THERE ARE LOTS OF STEPS AND A STREET CUTTING ACROSS.

TO GO UPHILL, YOU NEED TO CROSS THAT STREET SOMEWHERE.
A SNIPER PERCHED ON A HIGH SPOT CAN DOMINATE THE BATTLE.

FROM DOWN BELOW...
...THE HOUSES GET IN THE WAY, SO IT'S HARD TO AIM WHILE STAYING HIDDEN.
IT'S EVEN WORSE WHEN YOU DON'T HAVE THE RANGE.

TAMAKOMA HAS A POWERFUL SNIPER.
MAYBE IT'S THEIR PLAN TO TAKE THE HILL...?

HMM, I DON'T KNOW...
THERE'S A DIFFERENCE IN SNIPER PROFICIENCY.
THEY WON'T HAVE AN EDGE IN A NORMAL BATTLE.

WHAT ABOUT SUWA SQUAD, WHICH HAS NO SNIPER?
IT'LL BE SUPER HARD.
ESPECIALLY IF ANOTHER TEAM GETS ABOVE THEM.
I BET SUWA'S FLIPPING OUT RIGHT NOW.

Suwa Squad Strategy Room

HUH?!
CITY-SCAPE C?!

YOU GOTTA BE KIDDING ME! THAT MAP **SUCKS**!
WHY COULDN'T THEY JUST PICK A OR B?!

CITYSCAPE C...?!
Arafune Squad Strategy Room

THAT'S THE MAP THAT FAVORS SNIPERS.
WHY'D THEY PICK THAT ONE?
MAYBE IT'S THEIR FIRST TIME AGAINST SNIPERS.

IT HELPS.
US, ANYWAY.

WATCH OUT FOR TAMAKOMA-2'S SNIPER.

WE'LL DO WHAT WE USUALLY DO.
ROGER!

Tamakoma-2 Squad Strategy Room
BEGIN IN: 52 SECONDS

TADA
ALL RIGHT!
MATCHING UNIFORMS! AWESOME!
THIS IS WHERE IT ALL BEGINS!

OSAMU.
READY FOR YOUR DEBUT MATCH?
PHEW
I'VE BEEN RUNNING THINGS OVER SO MUCH IN MY HEAD THAT I'M GETTING CONFUSED.

WE DID ALL THE RESEARCH WE COULD AND CAME UP WITH A PLAN.
WE'LL BE ALL RIGHT.
DON'T WORRY ABOUT IT.

EVEN IF YOU LOSE, YOU WON'T DIE.
STICK TO THE PLAN YOU CAME UP WITH.
OKAY!

ALL RIGHT...
LET'S GO!
KEEN
BEGIN B-RANK WAR.

AND THERE THEY ARE!

EACH AGENT GETS DROPPED AT A RANDOM LOCATION...

...SPACED APART FROM EACH OTHER!

BAGWORM ON
BAGWORM ON
BAGWORM ON
BAGWORM ON
AAAAAND THE FOUR SNIPERS ACTIVATE THEIR BAGWORMS!
THEY'VE DISAP-PEARED OFF THE RADAR!
THE THREE SNIPERS ON ARAFUNE SQUAD...
...HEAD STRAIGHT FOR THE HILL, OF COURSE!
AGENT HANZAKI STARTED IN A LUCKY SPOT.
SUWA SQUAD GOES AFTER THEM!
AND TAMA-KOMA-2...

THEY DON'T GO AFTER THEM!

THEY PRIORITIZED MEETING UP!

THE START IS WHEN EVERYONE'S MOST VULNERABLE.

IT'S A GOOD IDEA TO MEET UP.

BUT AT THIS RATE...

...ARAFUNE SQUAD IS GOING TO PIN US FROM ABOVE!

I STARTED IN A BAD SPOT.

BETTER HURRY ...!

?!

T

UG

SUWA!
DON'T RUSH OUT.
YOU'LL DIE IF YOU DON'T STICK TO THE WALLS.
SHF
CLOSE CALL FOR AGENT SASAMORI!
GOOD PICKOFF ATTEMPT BY HOKARI.
SUWA SQUAD DODGED THAT, BUT NOW IT WILL BE DIFFICULT FOR THEM TO ADVANCE.
VERY NICE.
TUP
CAPTAIN ARAFUNE SLIPS PAST THEM IN THE MEANTIME!
THE ENTIRE ARAFUNE SQUAD IS UPHILL!
DANG.
THIS IS ANNOYING.
EVERYTHING'S GONE PERFECTLY SO FAR.

BLAM
BOOM
!
THEY FIRED?!
AMATEURS ...
YOU GAVE YOUR-SELVES AWAY!

BLAM
BLAM
BLAM
UNH!!
KRANG!!
AGAIN, CHIKA!
RIGHT WHERE THAT FLASH OF LIGHT WAS!
OKAY!

BOOM
WOW! THIS IS BASICALLY CANNON FIRE!
SURPRISINGLY, TAMAKOMA-2 GOES FOR A FIREFIGHT!
CAPTAIN AZUMA!
WHAT DO YOU THINK OF THIS?!
I GET IT...
TAMA-KOMA-2 IS AT A DISADVAN-TAGE.
EVEN WITH ALL THAT POWER, FROM BELOW, THEY CAN'T SEE ARAFUNE SQUAD.
EVERY TIME THEY FIRE, IT REVEALS THEIR POSITION.
ARAFUNE SQUAD CAN EASILY TARGET THEM FROM ABOVE.

EVEN WITH ALL THE SHIELDS THEY CAN MUSTER...
SKRANG
...IT'S ONLY A MATTER OF TIME BEFORE THEY CRUMBLE.
LIKE CAPT. AZUMA EXPLAINED ...
...TAMA-KOMA-2 IS GETTING WHITTLED DOWN!
WAS IT FOOLISH TO CHALLENGE THE PROS TO A SNIPING MATCH?!
NO...
THEY WEREN'T GOING FOR THE WIN.
WHAT ...?!
ARAFUNE, WATCH OUT!!
!

HA HA!
HEY, ARAFUNE!!
HNF!
TWO ON ONE, HUH?
WHOA!! SUWA SQUAD USED THE BLASTS...
...TO COVER THEIR ADVANCE ON ARAFUNE SQUAD!
THAT CANNON FIRE WAS TO PROVIDE COVER FOR SUWA SQUAD.
THEY FACTORED THEIR INABILITY TO BEAT ARAFUNE SQUAD IN A LONG-RANGE BATTLE INTO THEIR OVERALL STRATEGY.

BY CHOOSING THIS STAGE...

...AND GIVING ARAFUNE SQUAD AN OBVIOUS ADVANTAGE...

STAGE SET

CITYSCAPE C

...THEY CREATED A NATURAL ALLEGIANCE WITH SUWA SQUAD.

TAMA-KOMA-2...

...PUT A LOT OF THOUGHT INTO THIS URBAN BATTLE.

To Be Continued In **World Trigger 11**!

Rejected storyboards

The Dark History

The legendary rejected storyboard "Untitled"

This is the storyboard for the manga I drew before Elite Agent Jin, the prototype for World Trigger. This is my only storyboard to get rejected. I wanted it to remain hidden away, but my manager claimed that a lot of people enjoy seeing stuff like this, so he compiled these pages. I don't have time to make anything else and need to fill these two pages, so whatever.

■Konami and Jin: Only there for exposition.

The main character is Yuma Kai. Not a shrimp. Neighbors were called Guests, but otherwise it was mostly the same.

■Triggers were mostly the same. The combat bodies were more sci-fi.

There were many named characters but not much character development with a ton of exposition. There was also a pointless narrative trick that misrepresented the time in the manga. It was the thing that made Bapti say, "It's so confusing," and "It's definitely boring."

■Osamu's prototype, Kengo Soma.

■Jin had a full-face mask.

■Usami was not cheerful.

Back then, I was trying something new. There were some romantic elements, but this is painful to look at. I'm an idiot. Well, my deadline has arrived, so I better wrap this up. I hope you enjoyed it at least a little bit.

WORLD TRIGGER

Bonus Character Pages

COMMANDER KIDO

Eyebrow Slit

The organization's leader, whose facial scar is often forgotten by the manga artist. The best medical staff available tried to restore his lost eyebrow, but nothing could be done. He demonstrated that he was actually able to stand up in this volume, but he is more intimidating while seated. So now the rumor is that he will always appear while being carried around in his chair.

MR. KARASAWA

Loves Rugby

He played rugby in school. He was well known back in the day as the calm and clear-minded fly half who orchestrated many great plays with a style that worked through even the smallest gaps in the opposing team's formation. He was raising funds for an evil organization until five years ago, but playing rugby got him recruited by Border. Even today his skills help him make astute observations in the conference room. His weakness is that he's a lightweight when it comes to alcohol.

MR. NETSUKI

Surprisingly Handy

The paragon of P.R. Since the beginning, he has existed to help other characters stand out. He went to the press conference perfectly prepared, but since he didn't play rugby in school, his plans were ruined by Mr. Karasawa and upstaged by Osamu. He would've been able to avoid this tragedy if he had only played rugby. His weakness is bad luck.

OSAMU'S MOM

Someone Give Her a Stick

A mother of one, who seems cool but is actually a close-range Attacker. She made passionate passes on her husband in college and got married right after graduation. The Mikumo household is a standard nuclear family. The son participates in the Rank Wars, the father goes overseas to build bridges and the mother goes down to the stream to do the laundry. But then a handy stick came floating down the stream, so the reporters should make a run for it. She's 39 and from the same graduating class as Netsuki.

OSANO

Lollipop Lucky Girl

An incomparable instinctive Operator. In junior high, she belonged to a talent agency and worked as a fashion model until she got bored and quit. The lollipop in her mouth comes from a stash Konami bought when she was tricked into believing they'd increase her bust size. They didn't work for Konami, but they did for Osano! The world smiles upon those free from greed, C-cup.

SAKURAKO

What Happened to Your Day Job?

She has patiently made presentations to the engineers and senior officers ever since she was a C-Rank and is the one who made the current Rank Wars broadcasting system. She's contributed greatly to training rookies and increasing Border's overall tactical levels. Her achievements are quite extraordinary. She likes melons and seasoned rice. She hates cilantro and praying mantises. Self-assessed B-cup.

YOU'RE READING THE WRONG WAY!

World Trigger reads from right to left, starting in the upper-right corner. Japanese is read from right to left, meaning that action, sound effects, and word-balloon order are completely reversed from the English order.

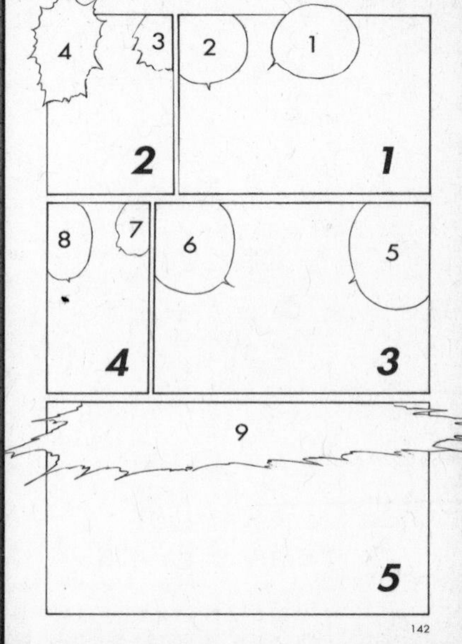